AF229602

Contents

Meet the Cook

My name is Ila Fern, and I am the main cook at Miller's Homestead Cooking. I've always been interested in working in the kitchen. As a young girl, I always liked making dinner, or supper, and enjoyed baking for the family.

Before I was married, I was excited to be hired by the Kalonial Townhouse restaurant in Kalona. I thought it was too much fun. I remember once telling a co-worker that it was too much fun to think that I was getting paid for doing something I loved.

The manager wondered how a young girl like myself could make such soft bread. I told him it was simple - I just made it the way my mom taught me.

Well, it wasn't long before I married my wonderful husband, Warren Dene, and we were blessed with three boys and five girls. The girls and I have had a lot of fun times together in the kitchen, with me teaching them the same way I was taught by my mom. We are also thankful for our grandchildren, and enjoy making their favorite foods and snacks, like Amish peanut butter. They are our little sunshines.

Now, I am happy to be cooking and serving meals for the guests of Miller's Homestead Cooking, along with my daughters, Megan, Monica, Michelle, Malana and Marsha. They are my right-hands and help me with pie baking, as well as all the other good things we make for our guests. If we need help with dishes or have more visitors than we six can handle, the guys help us out sometimes too.

All of our meals are served family style, meaning we fill up the bowls and you pass them around the table helping yourselves to the items and quantities that you want. We make sure you do not leave the table until you have had all you can eat.

While sharing our love of cooking, we have been blessed meeting a lot of people from all over the world. We enjoy hearing about how folks outside our Amish community live, and teaching them a little about why we love the simple life of an Amish farm family. You may enjoy some of our favorite anecdotes about our different lifestyles at the back of the book.

I have been asked by many people who come for the meals if I would consider teaching cooking classes. I thought about that, but finally decided it would be better to share my recipes, to make it easier for folks to return to their own homes and delight their own guests, who haven't have the opportunity to eat in our home.

I did not have exact measures for a lot of my recipes. I am one of those cooks that dumps, and makes guesses, until the items taste right or have the correct consistency. Printing this book has made me slow down, think about accurate measurements, and break down all the steps for beginners. We've tried to pare the recipes down to a size to fit a family, but those with the quilt symbol  also appear in a special section in the back with quantities to serve a crowd or a large family at the holidays.

So, browse through these tasty recipes and try something new for dinner. All of the recipes in the book are made from scratch. We hope you can find the same joy cooking these dishes as we do, and are sure your family and friends will savor the smell of home cooking in your own kitchen.

If you have any questions about the enclosed recipes, or other dishes you may have sampled at our home, please feel free to call me or my daughters. We will try our best to answer any questions that you have.

Hope you have a cookin' blast!

Ila Fern Miller - 319-461-2193
Miller Homestead Cooking
5708 Sharon Center Rd, Kalona, IA 52247

Warren & Ila Fern
Monica, Michelle, Malana, Milan, Mason, Marsha
Eugene & Megan, Kyler   Merle & Vera, Charity & Hope

Breads

Home Baked Bread

1 c. warm water	1½ T. lard	½ tsp. salt
2½ T. brown sugar	1¼ t. yeast	
⅓ c. prairie gold flour, rounded	2⅓ c. white flour	

Mix brown sugar, salt, lard and water until well blended. Stir in both flours and yeast. In a warm place, let rise in bowl for 30 minutes. Punch down and let rise again. Preheat oven to 350°. Separate into five loaf pans, greased with lard or butter. Let rise until double. Bake for 30-35 min. or until golden brown. Remove from oven, rub butter on top. Allow to cool 10 min. before slicing with a serrated blade (¾ inch thick.) Makes 1 loaf.
Tip: For a fine textured bread, dough should not be sticky. Add flour until smooth.
8   *Also, lard makes the best bread. Bread can be easily frozen.*

Monica's Dinner Rolls

2 c. milk
½ c. oil or lard
1/3 c. sugar
1 tsp. salt

2 eggs (beaten)
½ c. warm water
1 T. yeast
6 c. flour (+ 1c held back)

Scald milk, & blend with oil, sugar, salt and eggs. Cool to lukewarm Add rest of ingredients. Let rise in a warm place until double. Shape dough into 1½" balls. Place on well-greased 13x18" sheet pan. Preheat over to 350°. Let rise until double. Bake for 20-25 min until golden brown. Brush with melted butter. Makes approx. 35 rolls.
Tip: My favorite yeast is Saf-instant, available at Amish stores in Kalona. I put it on top of dry ingredients. You don't have to dissolve in warm water.

Butters

Easy Apple Butter

6½ c. applesauce
3⅓ c. sugar
1 tsp. cinnamon
⅛ tsp. cloves

⅛ c. water
⅛ c. vinegar
pinch of salt

Mix all ingredients well. Put mixture into a large roaster. Do not cover it. Cook mixture at 300º for 3½ hours. Stir vigorously every 15 minutes. Put in jars and store in freezer or refrigerator.
Makes 3½ pints.

The great taste of apple butter is only matched by the fantastic smell in your home.

Cinnamon Butter

1½ c. butter
1½ c. margarine
3 c. powdered sugar

3 tsp. cinnamon
¼ c. honey

Warm butter and margarine to ensure they are very soft. Combine all ingredients and beat until creamy. Serve on fresh dinner rolls.
Makes 3½ - 4 cups.

Marshmallow Creme

½ c. sugar

1 c. light Karo syrup

⅓ c. water

⅓ c. egg whites   1 tsp. vanilla

In heavy kettle, put sugar, water and ⅔ c. Karo and cook to a med. hard boil (240°). Do not undercook! Meanwhile in a bowl, place ⅓ c. warm Karo, egg whites and beat until fluffy. (You can hold the bowl upside down.) Remove 240° mixture from heat and pour in a fine stream into egg whites, beating all the while. Then beat hard for 2 minutes, and stir in vanilla. Place in air tight container to store once cool.

Make sure not to cover the creme until it is cold, or the condensation will ruin your treat.

Amish Peanut Butter 

18 oz. jar peanut butter   ⅔ c. light Karo syrup   ⅔ c. warm water
24 oz. Marshmallow Creme (previous page or store bought)

Mix peanut butter, karo and water well. Then fold in the marshmallow creme. Store in air tight container in refrigerator. Make 3 pints

After church services, most Amish have a noon meal together and this is a staple, served with fresh homemade bread. Some districts call it Amish church spread – we call it delicious!

Creamy Strawberry Butter

1 stick butter
½ c. powdered sugar

1 8-oz pkg cream cheese
1 c. strawberry jam

Cream butter and cream cheese together. Mix in powdered sugar and jam.
Beat well. Serve on fresh bread.
Makes 2½ cups.

Hint: I like to make sure the butter and cream cheese is at room temperature, and use a beater to make it whip up fluffier. We made this for our daughter's wedding and put in little cups at each place setting.

*Be Somebody
who makes Everybody
feel like a Somebody!*

*If God
is all you have,
You have all you need!*

No Cook Strawberry Jam

4 c. fresh strawberries ½ c. Instant DuraJel
3 c. sugar

Prepare fresh berries by removing stems, washing and chopping into fine pieces. Mix sugar and DuraJel together, then stir in prepared fruit. Let set on counter for 4 hours to thicken before eating. Refrigerate after serving. Excess can be stored in the freezer in air tight containers Makes 3 pints.

Tip: Most Amish stores have the Instant DuraJel.

Strawberry Rhubarb Jam

5 c. rhubarb, diced   3½ c. sugar
1 box strawberry gelatin

In a large saucepan, mix rhubarb and sugar, cooking over medium heat until mixture bubbles. Reduce heat, and let set for 1 hour, then bring to a roiling boil for 5 minutes. Turn off heat. Stir in gelatin. Put jam in jars and put lids on while hot. Seal jars and store. Makes 2½ pints.

This is my most popular jam. It definitely is a hit! I make double batches most of the time.

Fried Chicken

10 lbs. cut up chicken	3 T. butter & 3 T. canola oil
Flour	Lawry's seasoning salt & ground pepper

Heat large cast iron pan. Add canola oil and butter. Sprinkle chicken pieces with flour and fry on each side until skin is golden brown. Meanwhile, preheat oven to 300°. As pieces are browned, season with salt, pepper and Lawry's seasoning salt on each side, and place in roasting pan. Add more butter & oil to cast iron pan before browning next batch. When all pieces are browned, bake for 2 hours in covered roasting pan. Do not add water. Your chicken will come out nice and tender. Serves 10-12 people.

18   *Hint: I figure 1 lb chicken per person. We prefer fresh, not frozen.*

Roast Beef

10 lb arm roast   1 pkg dry onion soup mix

Preheat oven to 300°. Place roast in a casserole dish and sprinkle with soup mix. Do not add water. Cover with foil, making sure foil is well sealed around edges of dish. Bake for 5½ hours. For best results, do not peek. Remove from oven and let sit 10 minutes before slicing.
Serves approx. 20 people.

You will receive a lot of compliments when you serve this dish. It is a favorite and our most requested main dish.

Salisbury Steak

2 lb. hamburger	2 c. saltine cracker crumbs
2 tsp. salt & ½ tsp. pepper	2 sm onions (chopped) 2 cups milk
Sauce: 1 cup milk	8-oz can cream of mushroom soup

Mix first 6 ingredients well and form into loaf. Store overnight in refrigerator. Slice into ¾" steaks. In a cast iron pan, fry steaks in cooking oil and butter. Preheat oven to 300°. Stagger browned steaks in a baking dish. Mix cream of mushroom soup and 1 cup milk, then pour over all the pieces. Bake covered for 2 hours. Makes approx. 10-12 steaks

We quadruple this recipe in 9x13" and 9x9" pans to feed groups of 50.

Oven BBQ Pork Ribs

1 c. tomato juice	3 T. vinegar	⅓ c. brown sugar
1 onion, minced	½ tsp. paprika	½ tsp. chili powder
1½ tsp. ground mustard	½ c. ketchup	1 tsp. salt
3½ T. Worcestershire sauce	1 T. lemon juice	4 lb. pork ribs

Preheat oven to 300°. In a medium sauce pan, combine first 10 ingredients, and cook for 5 minutes stirring constantly. Remove from heat. Stir in lemon juice and allow to cool. Place ribs in a baking dish, and pour mixture over the top. Cover and bake for 5½ hours until tender. Serves 8

We made this for a special event and received rave reviews from the guests. One table passed the plate three times, so serving depends on appetitites.   21

Baked Ham

10 lb. bone in spiral ham   2 cups water

Preheat oven to 300°. Place ham in roaster. Add water and bake for 2 hours. Place foil over the roaster, sealing edges tightly to preserve moisture. Serves 15-20.

Tip: I like to cut the ham before baking, then it will be hot and ready to serve.

Meatloaf

3 lb. hamburger
½ tsp. garlic powder
2 tsp. chili powder
Sauce: 1 c. brown sugar
½ tsp. garlic powder

2 c. quick oatmeal
½ tsp. pepper & 1 tsp. salt
½ onion, diced
2 c. ketchup
1 T. Liquid Smoke

2 c. milk
2 eggs

Preheat oven to 300˚. Mix first 9 ingredients and form into loaf or press into a 9x13" pan. Pour sauce over top. Bake uncovered for 2 hours or until set, and new juices do not come to the top. Let set in oven for 10-15 min. after oven is turned off. Slice ½-¾" thick. Serves 15-18.
We make this annually for a third grade field trip. The kids love it with mashed potatoes and noodles.

Potatoes

Mashed Potatoes

10 lbs. Kennebec potatoes	2 qt. water	1 stick butter
1 stick cream cheese	3 tsp. salt	2 c. milk

Peel potatoes, quarter and put in an 8 qt. kettle. Add water and cook until soft. Drain. (Don't forget to set aside potato water for quick thickening gravy.) Add cream cheese. Mash potatoes until lumps are gone, then add butter and salt. Add milk in increments until you attain the right consistancy. Serves 18-20.

Hint: Adding cream cheese first and beating well will hinder lumps. For a different twist, brown butter and pour over mashed potatoes instead of gravy.

     Yum!

Chicken Gravy

Drippings from fried chicken
1½ c. cold water
Salt & Pepper

Water drained from potatoes
2 heaping T. flour

Strain the drippings from the baked chicken and place in stew pan. Add enough potato water to accomodate the size of crowd you are serving and heat to boil. In a gravy shaker, mix water and flour thoroughly. Slowly add flour mixture into drippings broth with a wire whisk, stirring constantly until gravy is thick. Season with salt and pepper to taste.

Roast Beef Gravy

Drippings from beef roast
1½ c. cold water
Salt & Pepper to taste

Water drained from potatoes
2 heaping T. flour

Strain the drippings from the dish where you baked your roast and transfer to a sauce pan. Add enough potato water to accomodate the number you are serving and heat thoroughly. In a gravy shaker, mix water and flour well. Slowly add flour mixture to your drippings broth with a wire whisk stirring constantly until gravy is thickened. Season with salt and pepper to taste.

   This is a crowd pleaser and my personal favorite!

Salisbury Steak Gravy

Drippings from browned steak
1½ c. cold water
Salt & Pepper to taste

Water drained from potatoes
2 heaping T. flour

After the steaks are done baking, strain some of the drippings and add to a stew pan. Add enough potato water to accomodate your guests and heat thoroughly. In a gravy shaker, mix water and flour thoroughly. Slowly add flour mixture to your drippings broth with a wire whisk, stirring constantly until gravy is thickened. Season with salt and pepper to taste.

A lot of people like the gravy over potatoes, topped with noodles.
Give it a try for a change of pace. Yummy!

Egg Noodles

3 c. egg yolks   1½ c. hot water
11 c. flour

Mix these three ingredients well. Roll up into logs and slice like cookies. Feed through the noodle maker. Lay on tables to dry for one week. Then place in air tight containers for storage, until you are ready to cook.

Tips: Noodles keep longer if you freeze them first, then store in a cool room. Using only yolks makes a richer color to your noodles.

Cooked Noodles for a Family

12 oz. pkg dried noodles

1⅔ qt. water

¾ c. chicken broth

1½ t. salt

¼ c. chicken base, or chicken & noodle seasoning

In a saucepan, add water, salt, seasoning and broth, and bring to a boil. Add dried noodles and bring to a boil again, then turn off burner. Let set for 30 minutes to 1 hour. The noodles will have absorbed all the liquid. Stir up and enjoy. This serves 12-14 people.

If you aren't feeding an army, you can pick up a package of dried Amish made noodles at many stores in and around Kalona, and serve this to your family.

Bread Dressing

2½ qt cubed bread (1loaf)   1 c diced celery   3 c Milk
2 T. chicken base   1 qt chicken broth with meat
1 T. seasoned salt   4 eggs (beaten)   ¼ t. black pepper
½ c browned butter   ⅓ c. diced onions

Preheat oven to 350.° In a small skillet, brown butter. Put bread cubes in a large bowl, and pour butter over top. Mix in seasonings and rest of ingredients. Pour into 9x13" baking pan, and bake for 1 hour or until golden brown. Serves 15-20.

*Everyone
you meet deserves
to be greeted with a smile*

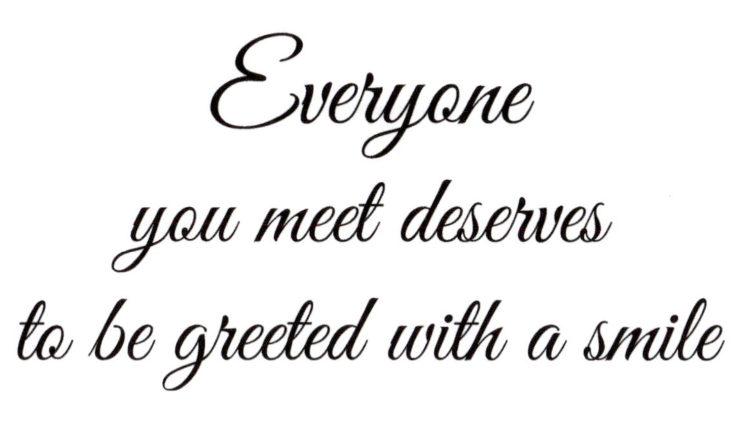

*The Journey
is just as important
as the destination*

Fresh Green Beans

Fresh Green Beans
Salt & Pepper

Olive Oil

Harvest or buy fresh green beans. Snap them and wash well. In a large kettle, place snapped beans and drizzle with olive oil. Season with salt and pepper. Heat on medium temperature with a lid on until tender, stirring occasionally.

Tip: Do not add water. You will lose the flavor if you do. People who say they don't like green beans are surprised to find they like these. Our family prefers to the beans long, unsnapped. Give that a try!

Mixed Vegetables

5 c. water   1 pkg. mixed frozen vegetables
2 T. butter   1 tsp. salt and ¼ tsp. pepper

In a small stew pan, add the butter. Cook over low heat, stirring frequently. When butter turns golden brown, remove from heat immediately.

In a saucepan, bring water to a boil. Add your choice of veggies. When they come to the top, drain using a strainer. Add the browned butter, salt and pepper to taste.

Sweet Corn

8 c. fresh sweet corn (18 ears)   2 c water
1 stick butter   2 tsp salt

Strip leaves and silk from ears of corn, submerge in cool water and brush
remaining silk off. Remove from water, allow to strain dry, and cut kernels
off the cob. We like the corn cutter we got from Pampered Chef. In a kettle with a lid, add all ingredients. Cook and stir for 5 minutes until tender.
Serves 16-18.

If storing for later, put kettle in ice water to cool immediately after cooking.
Spoon cooked corn into Ziploc bags and freeze. To reheat, empty bag into kettle
34   *over low heat and cook until hot.*

Fresh Peas

5 c. water

2 T. butter

1 qt. fresh shelled garden peas

1 tsp. salt & ¼ tsp. pepper

In a a large saucpen, heat water to boiling. Add your peas (frozen can also be used). When they come to the top, drain using a strainer. Add butter, salt and pepper to taste. Serve immediately.

These simply melt in your mouth.

Strawberry Tapioca Salad

12 c. water

2 c. sugar

2 c. cream, whipped, or 3-8 oz. cool whip

2 c. chopped fresh strawberries

2 c. tapioca

1 c. strawberry gelatin

In a large saucepan, bring water to a boil, then add tapioca, cook for 10-15 on then let set until soft. Add sugar and jello and reheat, sitrring constantly. Remove from heat and cool. Stir in whipped topping and strawberries. Serves 20-25 people.

Our most requested tapioca flavor, guests also like it for a lighter weight dessert alternative.

Garden Salad

1 head iceberg	1 head romaine
1 c. shredded carrots	2 c. shredded cheese
2-3 tomatoes, diced	crumbled bacon, optional
Dressing: 2 c. miracle whip	1 c. sour cream
1/2 tsp. salt	1 T. sugar

Shred and toss lettuce with carrots. Mix dressing ingredients and store in refrigerator, until ready to serve. Place lettuce mixture in bowl and drizzle with dressing, stirring slightly. Sprinkle on cheese and top with tomatoes and bacon. Serves 20-25.

Tip: More or less dressing can be used according to taste.

Orange Tapioca Salad

12 c. water
2 c. sugar
2 cans of mandarin oranges

2 c. tapioca
1 c. orange gelatin
2 c. cream or 3-8 oz. cool whip

In a large saucepan, bring water to a boil, add tapioca and cook for 10-15 minutes on high. Turn off heat and let set until soft. Add sugar and jello and reheat, sitrring constantly. Remove from heat and cool. Stir in whipped topping, and oranges. Serves 20-25.

2 cups fresh peaches, chopped, with peach gelatin makes another nice flavor alternative or 1½ cups crushed pineapple is another option!

Snicker Tapioca

4½ c. water
1⅛ c. baby pearl tapioca
¾ tsp. salt
1 c. brown sugar
2 T. butter

2 eggs, beaten
¾ c. milk
1½ T. vanilla
3 lg. or 6 sm. Snicker bars, diced
2-8 oz. tubs whipped topping

In a large saucepan, bring water to a boil, add tapioca and salt, cook for 10-15 minutes on high until tapioca is pliable. Add brown sugar, butter, eggs, milk, and vanilla. Bring to a boil, remove from heat and allow to cool. Stir in whipped topping and candy bars. Serves 15-18

At Christmas time, there are many requests for this one of a kind favorite. **39**

Cranberry Salad

10 oz. bag cranberries, thawed
3 apples, crushed
20 oz. can pineapple, drained

2 oranges, sectioned
1 c. sugar
2-6 oz. boxes raspberry jello

Grind fruit. Fix jello according to directions on box. Blend in ground fruit & remaining ingredients until well mixed. Refrigerate until ready to serve. Serve 40.

A Thanksgiving special, we grind the fruit with a crank grinder, but you could use a food processor,.

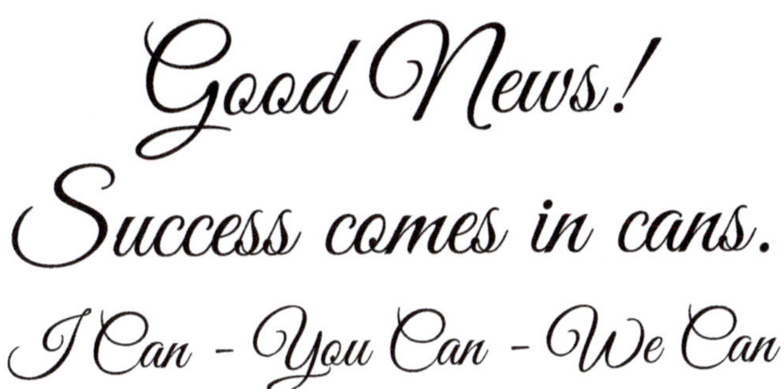

A Smile
is a powerful weapon.
You can even break ice with it.

Date Pudding

Batter: 1 c. dates, chopped   1 c. water   1 egg
½ c. chopped pecans   1 tsp. butter   2 tsp. soda
1 c. sugar   1½ c. flour+ 1 tsp. salt   1 tsp. vanilla
Sauce: 1 c. brown sugar   4 eggs, beaten   ½ c. flour
2 c. water   ½ c. butter   1 tsp. vanilla

Preheat oven to 350°. In a large bowl, soften dates by covering with boiling water for 10 minutes. In a separate bowl, mix remaining ingredients. Stir in dates/water and spread in 9 x 13" pan. Bake 30 minutes or until brown. Allow to cool. Serve in bowls by layering chunks of cake with sauce, then top with whipped cream and a sprinkling of nuts. Serves 20-25.

Graham Cracker Fluff

5 T. butter	7 T. sugar	3¼ c. graham cracker crumbs (30)
Filling: 1¼ c. sugar	2¼ c. milk	5 eggs, separated
5 c. Cool Whip	2 t. Vanilla	2 T. plain gelatin ¾ c water

Crush graham crackers, and cream together with sugar and butter. Press half the crumbs in bottom of 9x13" container. Beat egg yolks and set whites aside. Mix gelatin with water. In a large saucepan, bring milk, sugar and egg yolks to a boil for 1 minute, stirring constantly, then add gelatin and vanilla. Allow to cool while whipping the egg whites. Just before heated mixture sets up, whip in egg whites and whipped topping. Allow to cool, then spread filling on top of crumb base, and top with remaining crumbs. Refrigerate before serving. Serves 15-20.

Pies

Pie Crust

5 c. flour

½ tsp. salt

1½ c. lard or 1⅔ c. shortening

1 c. water scant

4 tsp. sugar

½ tsp. baking powder

2 eggs yolks

In a large bowl, mix dry ingredients with lard until dry and crumbly. Beat egg yolks in a 1 cup measuring cup & fill with cold water. Empty egg water into bowl and mix only until blended. For the flakiest crusts, make sure you do not overmix. Separate into 8 balls, and on a floured surface, roll ball into a circle, and place in pie pan. Prick with fork, and bake crusts for no bake pies at 350° for 15 minutes or until brown. Makes 8 crusts.

 See the next page for more hints on making great tasting pies!

Our Tips for Making Great Pies

Only pre-bake crusts for the cold cream pies.
We make the large recipe, and place extra crusts in the freezer
until needed. Just thaw and bake, then fill with your favorite filling.
Other pie shells should be unbaked until filling is added.
Bake at 350° until edges are golden.

To ensure your filling stays in the pie, always wet the outside edge of the
bottom crust before adding the top crust and lightly pinch closed.
Prick bottom of cream pie crusts with a fork or vent the top crusts
of two crust pies with a pair of kitchen shears. About 8 holes will do it.

Always sprinkle sugar on the top crust of double crust pies
before baking to sweeten the pie.

You can cut
pies into
6 or 8 pieces
depending
on the
appetite
of your crowd.

Peach Pie

6 c. peaches, sliced (frozen or fresh)   4½ c. water
⅛ tsp. salt   1½ c. sugar
Scant 1 c. perma-flo   1 T butter
1/8 c. orange & 1/8 c. peach jello

Preheat oven to 350°. In a large saucepan, mix 3 c. water, sugar and salt and bring to a boil. Mix 1½ c. cold water with perma-flo and add to boiling water, stirring constantly until thick and clear. Turn off heat. Mix in jello and when well mixed, stir in peaches. Spread into 2 unbaked pie crusts, top with another crust, and sprinkle with sugar. Bake until crust is golden and filling is set. Makes 2 pies that serve 12 - 16.

Cherry Pie

6 c. cherries
2 c. sugar
⅔ c. water
⅓ stick oleo

5½ c. water
1 c. perma-flo
⅓ c. cherry jello

Preheat oven to 350°. In a large saucepan, mix water, and sugar and bring to a boil. Mix perma-flo with water and add to the mixture. Return to a good boil, then add jello, butter and cherries. Spread mixture into 3 unbaked pie crusts, top with another pie crust and sprinkle with sugar. Bake at 350 until crust is golden. Makes 3 pies that will serve 18-24.

Apple Pie

1¼ qt. Jonathan apples, chopped
1 T. instant Dura-Jel, heaping

¾ c. sugar
1 t. cinnamon

Preheat oven to 350°. Mix dry ingredients together, then pour over apples and mix well. Pour into unbaked pie crust and top with another crust. Sprinkle top crust with sugar and bake until golden brown.
Makes 1 pie that serves 6-8.

The smell will fill your kitchen with a warm mouth watering scent.

Apple Crumb Pie

3¾ qt. apples, chopped
3 T. instant Dura-Jel, heaping
Crumb Topping: 2 c. flour
1 t. cream of tartar
1 t. baking soda

2½ c. sugar
3 t. cinnamon
½ c. sugar
½ c. butter

Preheat oven to 350°. Mix dry ingredients together, then pour over apples and mix well. Pour into unbaked pie crust Instead of using a top crust, in a large bowl, mix the crumb topping ingredients and crumble over the fillling. Bake 50-60 minutes until lightly browned. Makes 3 pies.

Expect your pies to crack on the top.

Ground Cherry Pie

2 c. water	1 c. sugar	2 c. ground cherries
pinch of salt	1 t. real-lemon	
3 T. Perma-Flo	½ c. water	

Preheat oven to 350°. In a saucepan, bring the ground cherries, water and sugar to a slow boil. Slowly stir in a mixture of water and perma-flo. Cook until thick, stirring frequently. Stir in real-lemon. Pour into an unbaked pie crust and dot with butter. Put a second crust on top and sprinkle with sugar. Bake 50 - 60 minutes, until golden brown. Makes 1 pie.

Ground cherries are grown on a plant in our garden, not on a tree, so this is not at all like a traditional cherry pie. They resemble wild chinese lanterns, which are poisonous.

Fresh Strawberry Pie

1 c. sugar
Pinch of salt
2 T. Karo syrup
1 qt. fresh strawberries

1 c. water
2 T. Perma-flo, rounded
2 T. strawberry jello
2 ½ c. whipped topping

In a large saucepan, mix sugar, water, salt, Perma-flo and Karo syrup together and cook until thick. Add jello and cool. Blend in 1 qt. fresh sliced strawberries. Spoon into a baked pie shell and top with whipped cream. Refrigerate before serving. Makes 1 pie.

We top with sliced strawberries for an attractive treat.

Rhubarb Meringue Pie

Filling: 2 c. rhubarb, diced   3 T. flour, rounded   1 c. sugar
1 c. heavy milk or cream   2 eggs, separated
Meringue: 2 egg whites   ¼ t. cream of tarter   ¼ c. sugar

Preheat oven to 350°. Place rhubarb in an unbaked crust. In a large bowl, separate eggs and sit whites to the side. Beat yolks to a froth. Mix in sugar and flour, and then blend in milk. Pour mixture over rhubarb. Bake pie for 50-60 min, until almost set, you don't want it shaky. Meanwhile, beat egg whites with cream of tartar until partly stiff. Add sugar, a little at a time, beating until stiff and glossy. Top hot filling with meringue, and return to oven for 15 minutes, until the meringue peaks are golden brown.

52   Makes 1 pie that serves 6-8.

Strawberry Rhubarb Pie

2 c. rhubarb, diced

1 c. sugar

½ c. water

2 c. strawberries, sliced

½ c. Instant Dura Jel

Preheat oven to 350°. In a large bowl, combine berries & rhubarb. In a second bowl, mix sugar and Dura Jel. Pour over fruit and blend until fruit is well coated. Add water and mix well. Spread fruit mixture in an unbaked pie crust and top with small dabs of butter. Add top pie crust, sprinkling with sugar. Bake 50-60 minutes until golden. Makes 1 pie that serves 6-8.

Rhubarb is one of the first signs of spring. These rhubarb pies are a favorite of our family for both the flavor and the advent of warmer weather to come. **53**

French Rhubarb Pie

1 egg
1 c. sugar
1 t. vanilla
Topping: ¾ c. flour
1/3 c. butter

2 c. diced rhubarb
2 Tbsp. flour
½ tsp. salt
½ c. brown sugar

Preheat oven to 350°. Mix egg, rhubarb, sugar, flour, vanilla and salt. Put rhubarb mixture into an unbaked pie shell. Combine topping ingredients and crumble over filling. Bake for 40 minutes or until golden brown. Makes 1 pie that serves 6-8.

Pecan Pie

3 eggs (slightly beaten)   1 T. melted butter
1 c. sugar   ½ t. salt
1 c. light corn syrup   1 t. vanilla
1 c. pecans   1 T. flour

Preheat oven to 350°. In a large bowl, blend eggs, butter, sugar, salt, corn syrup and vanilla. Mix flour with nuts and fold into mixture. Pour into unbaked pie shell. Bake 50-60 minutes until almost set - filling can shake a little. Makes 1 pie that serves 6-8.

This very tasty pie is great with ice cream!

Vanilla Crumb Pie

Filling: ¾ c. brown sugar • 3 T. (heaping) flour • ¾ c. white sugar
2 pints cold water • 2 c. light corn syrup • 2 eggs, well beaten
3 tsp. vanilla
Crumb Topping: 2 c. flour • 1 tsp. cream of tartar • ½ c. sugar
½ c. butter (softened) • 1 tsp. soda

Preheat oven to 375°. In a large saucepan, beat eggs well, then mix in flour, sugars, water, and syrup. When well blended, bring to a boil. Remove from heat. Stir in vanilla. Pour into 3 unbaked pie shells. Cream the topping ingredients. Crumble over filling. Bake until brown. Makes 3 pies.

  The older generation know and love this pie.

Pumpkin Pie

⅓ c. flour
2 eggs, separated
¼ tsp. nutmeg

½ c. pumpkin
⅛ tsp. allspice
2 c. milk

¼ tsp. salt
¾ c. sugar
½ tsp. cinnamon

Preheat oven to 350°. Divide eggs, and set aside whites. Beat yolks, add sugar, flour and spices. In a large saucepan, heat milk until it gets a skin. Add milk to pumpkin mixture. Beat egg whites until frothy and fold in last. Spread in an unbaked pie shell and sprinkle with cinnamon. Bake until filling is set (it isn't shaky) approx. 45-50 min Makes 1 pie that serves 6-8.

Amish pumpkin pie is different than most folks are used to, but it is our family's favorite for the fall.

Chocolate Cream Pie

3 c. milk	2 eggs	1 c. sugar
½ c. Perma-Flo Starch	½ tsp. salt	½ tsp. vanilla
2 T. cocoa	1 chocolate bar	2½ c. whip topping

In a large saucepan, heat milk to scalding. In a separate bowl, beat eggs and add sugar, cocoa, perma-flo and salt. Add slowly to the hot milk and stir until thick. Remove from heat and add vanilla. Chill for 20 minutes and scoop into a baked pie crust and top with whipped cream. Grate chocolate bar over the top. Makes 1 pie.

Raisin Cream Pie

1 c. raisins
2 eggs
½ c. Perma-Flo Starch

½ c. water
1 tsp. vanilla
¾ c. sugar

1T. butter
2½ c. milk
⅛ tsp. salt

In a saucepan, mix raisins, water and butter and bring to a boil. In a large stew pan, mix remaining ingredients, and then blend into the cooked raisin mixture. Cook until thick. Put into a baked pie crust and top with 2½ c. whipped topping. Makes 1 pie which serves 6-8.

This is an old-time favorite – but only for those who like raisins.

Coconut Cream Pie

3 c. milk
2/3 c. sugar
½ tsp. salt
½ c. coconut shredded + some to sprinkle

2 eggs
½ c. Perma-Flo Starch
½ tsp. vanilla

In a large saucepan, heat milk to scalding. Beat eggs and add sugar, salt and perma-flo. Mix well. Pour mixture slowly into hot milk and cook until thick. Add vanilla and coconut. Chill. Put into a baked pie crust and top with whipped cream. Sprinkle with coconut. Makes 1 pie that serves 6-8.

This is our #1 cream pie.

Peanut Butter Pie

Filling: 3 c. milk   2 eggs   ¾ c. sugar
½ c. Perma-Flo Starch   1 t. vanilla   ½ tsp. salt
Topping: 2½ c. whipped topping
Crumb Topping: ⅓ c. peanut butter   1 c. powdered sugar

In a large saucepan, heat milk. While that is heating, mix eggs, sugar, salt and perma-flo. Pour this mixture into the hot milk and cook over heat until thick. Add vanilla. Chill. Line bottom of baked pie crust with ¾ c. crumb mixture. Top with a layer of filling, then a layer of whipped topping, finally sprinkle the remaining crumbs on the top. Makes 1 pie.

Everyone likes this one! The peanut butter taste is light and yummy.   61

Lemon Pie

1 c. sugar, scant	¼ c. real lemon juice	1½ c. water
⅓ c. Perma-Flo Starch	1½ t. lemon flavoring	3 T. butter
3 eggs, separated		
Meringue: 3 egg whites	¼ t. cream of tarter	¼ c. sugar

In a large saucepan, bring sugar, water and perma-flo to a boil for 1 min. In a separate bowl, separate eggs, and beat egg yolks. Stir yolks into hot mixture and boil 1 more minute. Remove from heat and add lemon juice, flavoring and butter. Put in a baked pie crust. Meanwhile, beat egg whites with cream of tartar until partly stiff. Add sugar, a little at a time, beating until stiff and glossy. Top filling with meringue, and brown meringue under broiler until peaks are golden brown. Makes 1 pie.

Banana Cream Pie

3 c. milk	2 eggs
2/3 c. sugar	½ c. Perma-Flo Starch
½ tsp. salt	½ tsp. vanilla

In a large saucepan, heat milk to scalding. In a bowl, beat eggs, then add sugar, perma-flo and salt. Add sugar mixture slowly to the hot milk and cook until thick. Add vanilla. Allow to cool. Line a baked pie shell with sliced bananas, fill with pudding mixture and top with whipped cream. Slice bananas to garnish the top. Makes 1 pie that serves 6-8.

Shoo-fly Pie

Filling: 2 eggs, beaten   ¼ c. brown sugar   1 c. molasses
1 c. boiling water   ½ tsp. soda
Crumb Topping: 1½ c. flour   ½ c. brown sugar
¼ tsp. soda   1 c. lard

Preheat oven to 300°. Cream crumb topping ingredients and set aside. Blend filling ingredients, then stir in 1 cup of crumb mixture. Divide filling into 2 unbaked pie crusts. Top with remaining crumbs. Bake 60 min, until golden. Pie is done when you cannot poke it down. (The crumb mixture it will feel firm not mushy.) Makes 2 pies.

This is a pie that Pennsylvania amish have to entertain guests. They also eat it for breakfast with coffee.

Large Group Recipes

Not everyone has a large group to serve, so the photographed recipes in the front of the cookbook were scaled back to accommodate a single family or group of 6-8 people. We marked some of those recipes with the quilt block symbol above. If you see that symbol, you will know the quantities for serving a large group are included back here in this section.
Happy Gathering!

Home Baked Bread (Five Loaves/ 60 Slices)

4½ c. warm water	½ c. lard	3 tsp. salt
¾ c. brown sugar	2 T. yeast	
2 c prairie gold flour, rounded	11 c. white flour	

Easy Apple Butter (14 pints)

26 c. applesauce	½ c. water
13½ c. sugar	½ c. vinegar
4 tsp. cinnamon	pinch of salt
½ tsp. cloves	

Amish Peanut Butter (10 pints)

3-18 oz. jar peanut butter   2 c. light Karo syrup   2 c. warm water
Marshmallow Creme (recipe page 12 or 3-24 oz store bought)

Cooked Noodles for a Crowd (75)

4 lb. noodles	9 qts. water
1 qt. chicken broth	3 T. salt

¾ c. chicken base, or chicken & noodle seasoning*

These are a must with each meal that we serve. We use the broth we strain off our baked chicken gravy drippings, and purchase the base or seasoning at several of the local Amish stores.

Shoo-fly Pie (7 pies/ 56 pieces)

Filling: 9 eggs, beaten	1 c. brown sugar	4 c. molasses
4 c. boiling water	2 tsp. soda	
Crumb Topping:	6 c. flour	2 c. brown sugar
1 tsp. soda	1 c. lard	

Humorous Happenings

In conversing with the folks who come to our farm for a home cooked meal, we are often reminded that we all have different life experiences. While Amish life seems strange to our visitors, some of their remarks seem very humorous to us. These are a few of our favorites.

We have a Daystar skylight in our dining area, which is a common way many Amish collect, amplify, and disperse natural sunlight. This system is so efficient, it seems like the electric lights used by the English, even on very cloudy days. We have had people who have requested us to turn off the lights. Well, we had to tell them, we can't - it is the sun!

People like to travel around our farm on buggy rides, and we often point out our farm animals. We have a dairy of 25 milking cows, and laying hens for eggs. We are tickled by some of the questions we get from the city folk, like:
"Are the milk cows boys or girls?"
"Are the brown cows the ones that give chocolate milk?"
"Do you sit inside or outside the buggy?" We all still giggle when we imagine how we would look riding on the roof.

A lady from the city came for farm fresh eggs. When we took her out to the chicken house, she wondered out loud where the eggs came from. Once we explained how the hens "laid" the eggs, she said, "Oh! I think I will go to the store to get my eggs."

These moments keep life interesting . . .

Another question we are often asked is, "How can you be content without TV and technology? Don't you wish for it?" Our response is since we have never had it, we don't miss it. We often hear our guests discussing their busy and hectic lives, and that reminds us to be thankful for our heritage - our plain and simple way, embracing our family around us, and God who has blessed us.

Be a little person
who makes a
big difference

The things you take
for granted
someone else is
praying for.

Taste of Amish

The Kalona Amish community is
famous for their German style cooking.
Making use of the organic meats raised locally,
the fare is served up family style in
large serving dishes passed around the table.
The fresh fruits and vegetables
grown in gardens and greenhouses in the area
ensure you enjoy the tastiest salads and
desserts to top off your dining experience.
It's no wonder folks come from miles around
and even over seas to experience
an Amish home cooked meal.

This cookbook features some of the most popular
Amish dishes for you and your family to enjoy.
These diverse and delicious recipes are the
next best thing to having an Amish woman
cooking in your kitchen.